Writings from
Oneness

Writings from Oneness

Ian McCall

BOOKS

Winchester, UK
Washington, USA

First published by O-Books, 2011
O-Books is an imprint of John Hunt Publishing Ltd., Laurel House, Station Approach,
Alresford, Hants, SO24 9JH, UK
office1@o-books.net
www.o-books.com

For distributor details and how to order please visit the 'Ordering' section on our website.

Text copyright: Ian McCall 2010

ISBN: 978 1 84694 437 6

A CIP catalogue record for this book is available from the British Library.

Design: Stuart Davies

Printed in the UK by CPI Antony Rowe
Printed in the USA by Offset Paperback Mfrs, Inc

We operate a distinctive and ethical publishing philosophy in all
areas of our business, from our global network of authors to
production and worldwide distribution.

CONTENTS

Acknowledgement

Thank you

Dad, for Kipling's "If" and love.

Frank, for telling me about Ego before I could understand it.

Pete, for the brother who desired nothing in the end except
being together.

Mum for love and support.

Steve and Eleni for walking your own path

John for friendship.

Dave for walks in Calderstones Park on Sunday mornings.

Clive Laybourn, for tales of the Himalayas and hippies.

Maitreya for samadhi, Oneness and all you taught me.

Samadhi (ne Sarah) for beauty of stillness.

John and Jill for samadhi and passion.

Joseph for help and for love.

Esther for love and healing.

Rose for love and showing me so much.

Janet for love and escape from the dross.

Gavin Swabey for being a good soul.

Sue for innocence.

Dave, Ian, Colin and mates in Gamlingay.

Zoë for love and that which cannot be said.

Everyone and everything, for all that is.

Introduction

Welcome. This book is a collection of prose and poems written for a weekly Self Realisation group, sometimes referred to as a Meditation group. It is not, of course, a substitute for meditation, awareness or meeting and spending time with people who are awake - but rather an aid. I know there are people in the world with a real and sometimes profound interest in being Awake - and if you, the reader are one of them - then this has been written primarily for you from my heart. The awakened state of being is the natural state of being and from it comes natural love untainted. The World needs love.

Some teachers in this field have prided themselves in being clever or "kick-ass", blasting or verbally assassinating aspirants. I did not feel this was necessary or right; nor am I an all-knowing person who is much different from you the reader. I would ask you to read it carefully with a genuine openness. Question, if you will, what is written and look at things yourself. Go into it properly, if you will, and see if it works. You may find some of it challenging so bear with me if you can when reading it or putting it into practice.

You'll notice reference to terms like "Oneness" and "Ego". I hope you will, at the least, get a sense of what "Oneness" is and it is no good me trying to explain it now. By "Ego" I mean ego in the Yogic or Buddhist sense, that is, a false impression of what we are, or an illusory conditioned self which distorts how we see things.

However well (or unwell!) a book is written, in the field you are in now, it will probably not be enough: the writings are designed to help us put being awake into practice; please do this if you will and I think it will work better. It is good to have some sort of support network if you are in earnest about going into it and finding the truth. Ideally, a good teacher and in addition someone who is at the least as open as you are, with whom you can talk without fear, about awareness, meditation and related matters. At the time of writing I run a little group in Lincoln, England, open to anyone of genuine interest. I also run retreats, which I would thoroughly recommend for anyone genuinely interested in being Awake. No prerequisite is required except openness to Love, Truth and Oneness. Being with other people without Ego is an amazing gift for all and this is what the retreat aims to offer amongst other things. Be wary of charlatans and ego maniacs in this field: it can be dangerous on occasion.

I wish you all the best for your True Being. And I wish you love, truth and oneness.

With Thanks
Ian McCall

WELCOME

Welcome us all

Welcome to Love

Welcome to Truth

Can we travel together?

To a place where there is no movement,

No pressure

No separation

Only Us, the one Self that we are

In the beauty of Oneness

That this Life is

Chapter One

Starting Here and Now

Do Not Worry
(No Time to Waste)

Do not worry about what you were
Or what you have done
Or what happened to you
Because, here, it does not matter
Surrender it all to the Universe
To Oneness and the True Self that you are
Be free of it
And be. Awakened and Pure

Living in Enlightenment

What is Enlightenment?
Being awake
Being here now
Being in Oneness

Which is
Being at home

How to Use The Tao

There are infinite ways to use the Tao
Your Will is free and yours, ultimately
Your desire is yours too, is it not?
How far do you want to go with it?

When you enter on the "path" consciously, it may be important to become aware of why we are entering upon this path or way of being.

Do we want to relax a bit more; do we want to learn to meditate and become more knowledgeable about it; do we wish to gain confidence through it?

Or are we looking for something more?

The Tao or "way of virtue" can offer different things to different people: some of these things are peripherals e.g. confidence. You may want to use the teachings to improve your self-confidence. Or some other peripheral.

Or, you may wish to go deeper. You may have come to a point in your life where you simply cannot go any further in the way that you have done so far. You may be sick of the ego with all its pain, shallowness, falseness and self-interest. You may even be sick of "spiritual paths".

If that is the case, the Tao may offer you something else: a coming home, a radical shift back to the centre of your being.

What you allow to happen is down to your own will. No matter what anyone tells you, you will only go as far as you allow yourself (by will).

If you sit in meditation for 14 hours a day but are not genuinely open to change, to a radical centering of perspective, then your time will be, in one sense, wasted. Of course you could argue to the contrary.

But I think it is safe to say, Will is crucial to you and the world benefiting deeply from the meditation and from the way of the Truth. Otherwise, no matter how adept you become in meditation or reaching particular states, these can only be achievements; something else for the ego to own.

Having said all that, it remains your decision: your Will is sacred (as ultimately all consciousness is); and you can decide for yourself and no-one can change that.

Be careful!

Identity

From what shall we take our identity?

From our profession?
Or from where we live?
From the car we drive or the bike we ride?

From how clever or stupid we appear?
From what we are thinking
From that which we are feeling
From this body, young, old or in-between?

From that which we eat
Or that we which we don't?
From how we think we appear
And that which others think or feel about us?

Or yet from another:
Seemingly formless
It is called:
Pure Self
Or pure consciousness

From Being Here now,

At home

How Do We Know?

How do we know?
If science is right?
If existence continues after death?
Where the chakras are?

Would it even help to know?
Isn't it better: to start here now.
And live.

Joy/Exploration

Walking along the river, head full
Lost in a dream that wasn't even good

Sat down on the bank
Ah, it was here all along:
How beautiful
I remembered, or something
Oh the folly, of forgetting I cannot understand it
But sweet joy of returning,
Bathed in the love of the Universe

Be not ruled by any idea of what we should be
Return to the awakened state:
Not knowing yet wise
Return to zero:
Loving and simple
Return to Truth:
No rules

On a trip together with humanity
Explore, discover together
Joy, Sadness
Love
Oneness

We Remember Our Infinity

I relax:
It's not about trying
There is no state to reach
What are states when compared to the
Majesty of the Self?

It's not about thinking this,
Getting-up at a particular time
Is it about love?

I remembered: that I don't really know what
I am
It cannot be said perhaps
Cannot be reached with the mind perhaps
For what is there to reach outside of our
Being now
Perfect and complete?

And what are we to each-other?
Are we so different?
Or are we the same thing
You and I:
Are we Us?
Sweet joy of existence
As One

Free

I am
Free
We are
Free
Being is pervading all
Free
I am love
We are love
Love flows freely

Happiness

What is happiness?

It will help our deepening of Being if we contemplate the meaning of happiness. Happiness is perhaps what most human beings desire. The desire for happiness is not necessarily right or wrong: it's just manifesting within our consciousness.

However, it may be beneficial to look into the matter and realise at a profound level what is occurring. The desire for happiness can become an aim, a goal. This could drive us to a particular end-result, desirable or otherwise.

If we desire something strongly enough we may fulfil that ambition, e.g. a new job with better pay, more respect from our peers and so forth. This may please us for some time but we may then realise the job, the money, the status is not making us happy: people are still rude and disrespectful to us; and despite the pay-rise we still have bills to pay and we see others earning far more.

We may come to a realisation that happiness will not come through more money and more status (of course many people do not get this far and they will continue their drive for advancement until they see through what is going-on, or until they die). Once we have made that realisation we will be wiser in that one area of our consciousness.

But the drive, the search for happiness or 'a bit more' is still there and may lead us to the next thing: a new relationship perhaps or a new place to live. A new partner may give that happiness but after time things do not seem so beautiful: my partner takes me for granted now; why aren't we in love the way we used to be?

If we are lucky, we may realise changing partners will not necessarily bring happiness either. At least not whilst we are living from the insatiable dialogue of the Ego.

Going through life making these understandings is beneficial yet time appears limited. How long have we got?

It seems there is not enough time in this life to go through each area of our desires in this way. So what do we do?

The Gentle Way

I was thinking about
How sad some people are:
Confusion, Madness and Illusion all around
I was feeling sad about how lost some people are

Then stillness
I remember what is here
We are at the controls

The tidal wave is carrying the world
It cannot be fought on its own terms
Though we can try
Simpler:
To give up the fight
To let it go
And surrender to Oneness, the pure consciousness

Only then can it be conquered

Being, the Purity of It

We are pure being

Sense it
Realise it
Remember it

What underlies the world of Ego illusion?
Oneness
What is the nature of Oneness?
Purity
Are you and I the same Being?

Full Time/Part Time

What is more important:
A new car, or a new love for all?
Status or love?
Beautiful things or a shining heart?
Advancement of career
Or spiritual awakening?

Stir the Self from its slumber
Wake up!
Start caring about what is important
If you don't know what is important – then find out

All around are part-timers
They are worried about the world
But they are busy right now with their own little world
"I'd like to help but there's a few things I've got to get
through first"
"I'd like to be enlightened – but it's easier for you, you haven't

got my commitments"

How long do you think there is?
How long will you be here in this life?
When you die, what will you say to yourself?
- "Yes, I put Love first, I put Truth first"
- Or
- "Oh shit, what was I thinking of?"

Be Careful be Loving

When you wake, and always,
Be careful

Be careful we do not deceive ourselves
Or trip off into illusions about ourselves
Or others

Be open always
But know faith can be a dangerous gate to open:
It if lets in that which is untrue

Be careful of glib answers
And people who seem to know everything,
imbued with attractive confidence as they may be

Be careful with those who assassinate others
What is their driving force?

Be wary of those who claim enlightenment
On whose authority?

Be careful with those who claim knowledge of the subtle
energies

Can they really 'see' them?
Or did they read it in a book?

Be careful when we judge
If we have to

Be careful of those judging others and implying their own
    righteousness

And yet be true to one's True Self
The Truth,
And to the Oneness
Which will nurture you

And from that truth be loving
In Oneness
One

This Life is Sacred

How much time is there?
And who knows?

Oneness,
All is here, now:
There is nothing to achieve or reach – because all is already
    here.
Trust the Oneness that one is
And share it with others.

Start in Oneness
Start from here now, in the centre of Being
Trust or Being is the way here
And Love is the natural condition

Ideals fade as Being takes the fore;
For in Oneness and True Self all is complete.
Trust then, Pure Self and Universe,
Most of all:
Trust the Oneness
Living with the Oneness, with the Tao
It will look after Us

Us

Truth is ultimately, Us
Love flows between us of its own accord
I is You
You is I
I is not more important or less important than We
The divine 'I' need not be denied
Likewise, the divine 'Us'
You are sacred
I is sacred
We are sacred

Can We Serve Two Masters?

Oneness is the absolute Truth pervading all.
Observe dispassionately: and it will be realised.
Abandon opinions and one will see with unpolluted eyes.
In absolute Truth, in Oneness, Ego does not exist.
What then is Ego?

Simply put it is illusion, a divine distortion of perception. It may
have a purpose – but that purpose has been served.

A time slot for Oneness and another for Ego is limitation. It
is the ego-illusion's bid for control.

For real realisation of Love, Truth and Oneness, our

awareness should be here, now eternally

Start from Oneness

It is simpler.

Years ago a friend was reading "A Course in Miracles". He told me that Romantic Love is an illusion based upon a "special relationship", itself based upon the ego. Of course, this may be largely true.

But just as complete spiritual fulfilment may not be found in the ego's romantic love, finding its opposite will not offer it either. This is 'Duality'.

It is beyond and below these.

These two things come from it.

Start in oneness if you will.

And if you will it not, well that's fine too:

For your will, like everything perhaps, is sacred.

It comes down to You

And Oneness

Being Honest About Consciousness

When I was staying in a spiritual community I noticed something unusual. Upon meeting people I would often ask them how they were. I nearly always got a reply like "great" or "good". I was quite pressured and often unhappy at that time so when asked in return how I was, I would say "great" or "pretty rough today – having a difficult time at work" or such. It seemed usually to go down like a lead balloon. My sense was that people disapproved of what they saw as personal or negative expressions. The teaching there emphasized negation of the Personal. There is a powerful message in this teaching – it can negate egotistical indulgence in how we are feeling or thinking. Noble as this may be, not telling someone if you feel troubled does not *necessarily* rid you of ego, just as its opposite may not.

Because: a fundamental change is what is required to relinquish ego. There are a lot of people in the New Age who present themselves as outwardly perfect or in control. This is why we get glib answers to questions; ideals and idealism. However, one's true self, is not an ideal but rather *a living reality* and there is a very profound difference if you look into this. Whatever you are aware of in your consciousness is what you are conscious of. Pure Being in Oneness is inherently perfect and allows all – it is honest with consciousness. Trying to stop particular feelings or thoughts is usually high vanity; it is ego and its attempts to control everything including the spiritual. Being and being free is not conditional or subject to control; nor is it limited by an ideal of how we should be, behave or think. Ego control has to be abandoned for the genuine seeker. Then our true nature, or true self in Oneness, can be left to take the reigns.

A fundamental change starts here now, in Oneness. Not in dualities.

Chapter Two

Passion for Oneness

Passion for Oneness

Passion in ego is impure
Cultivate then, a passion that is pure
A passion in our belly
A gentle and resolute passion:
For truth of being
For Being, simple
For love, devoid of ego-self
For joining together in Oneness
For Oneness

Passion and Practice

From inner stillness of Oneness comes Passion.
From this comes a sense of divine urgency.
Realising the pain and suffering that the ego perpetuates,
    cultivate a loving and gentle passion for being here now.
There is time for joy, for laughter and for sadness.
Practising being here now every moment.
A sense of divine urgency arises from realising we cannot go-
    on any longer in ego.
There is no time to waste in ego; for life is precious.
Being in the timeless moment now is Truth and is central to
    the natural life in Oneness.
The urgency must be realised.
Realising the urgency we see:
Practising Being in Oneness here and now comes first in all

we are and do.

Purpose:

Being, Here Now
Practice: loving All and Everything, within and without
Being, aware of thought impressions, feelings, memories and
    phenomena- and allowing them to Be, without discrimination
Listening with openness, gentleness and love
Alive, in Oneness

Risky

Oneness, the following of it,
Seems risky:

The ego likes to know,
To have a plan,
To follow what it thinks is safe
Because it knows not that which is unknowable to it

And love seems risky
Where will it take us?
Can we bear the heights it raises us to?
And do we really want the Truth it will bring us into?
Who will tell us what is right, what is wrong
When all has fallen away?
And we are in the perfect Samadhi
Of the beauty of being so alive,
So beautiful,
So vulnerable,
Suckling at the breast of the Mother,
The Father,
Brahma.

The Still Point

Karmas blowing around you
Ready to take you here and there
-Stay in the still point and leave the field of karma

Struggling and searching for Enlightenment
Concerned about reaching this and losing that
-Return to the still point and it's clarity

Robbed by your friend
Yet not quite understanding why
-Stay in the still point

The still point is where one really is
Underlying all
The still point is here now
 And it is always here
Within you
Use it.

Passion

"In this body, six feet or so in length, the world (of the Ego)
    begins, and the world can end"

There is great suffering, unbridled cruelty and destruction in
    the world of the ego

But there is great beauty of essential being underlying

There is great love underlying, binding
Cultivate, if you will, a great passion for the moment now
For love between us all, the One Self

Cultivate it, if you will, in your Life and together, in our Life, our Being

In Oneness

Chapter Three

A Brief Guide To Meditation

Realisation of Self and Oneness:
Simple Meditation

Introduction: what is meditation; what is its purpose; what is the ego?

Meditation: how to meditate; preparation; breathing; awareness.

Simple Meditation
Introduction

What is it?

People have meditated for a long time- at least thousands of years.

What then is meditation? Well there are many forms, some religious, some not, some structured and some not. To understand it as fully as we can, we need to keep things simple.

By looking at a very simple form of it we will find it easier to understand. True understanding can only come from you the reader, now.

Simply put, meditation is awareness of our true nature; awareness of the person we really are; awareness of reality. This reality is underlying the near constant ego chatter. It is a *near* constant chatter however, not a perpetual one. Our true nature is not some strange, odd person whom we do not know (though there are those who would like you to think that).

Because that person has always been here in the midst, in our centre; and is here now as you read this. That person is what you really are.

It should be noted that most people at the least have meditated in some form naturally, without trying.

Let us keep to simple meditation if you will- and forget for now about other things.

What is it for?

Meditation is designed to help us realise what we really are. And to allow that which we really are to be. And to allow that which we really are to come to the fore.

Generally, people do not spend much time looking at themselves. We may be too busy or have other more pressing things to do; we may be occupied making ends meet or looking after our family; we may even be afraid to look at what is going on in our consciousness.

Meditation allows us to "see" our true self or being. It also allows us to see the workings of the mind and what we call the ego or false self. Whether we have realised it or not, ego is causing immense suffering in the world at an individual, and at a collective level. Meditation also has many beneficial side-effects but as we are keeping things simple, we will leave them for now.

So, meditation will help us realise:

- What we really are
- What we really are not
- What the ego is
- What restricts us
- What makes us happy
- What makes us unhappy

The difference between our true nature and ego consciousness

What is the Ego?

Simply put, the ego, as we will use the word here, means a false impression of what we really are. If I said to you "I am superior to you because my car cost far more money than yours," then that would be ego: I am seeing myself through an idea about money, material and status; and I am devaluing you through the same mechanism. Of course the ego is often more subtle and hidden than this example. Do not worry if you do not understand it because that is where the meditation comes in handy.

Meditation. How to meditate: preparation; breathing; awareness

How to meditate.
Stage One, Preparation:

- Set aside undisturbed time
- Sit on a chair, stool or cushions
- Sit with your back straight
- Be as comfortable as you can
- Do not lean back on anything (if possible)
- Back and neck 'straight' and relaxed
- Relax the belly
- Breathe from your belly or diaphragm
- Close your eyes if necessary. If not, then keep them open or half-open. Allow the vision to go 'wide', or if this feels hard, then focus on a point about 6 feet ahead on the floor or wall. Do not bow your head.

Stage Two, Concentration:

Now focus your attention gently upon your belly; more exactly, about 2 inches below your navel and about 2 inches inward, the

'Hara'. Gently allow yourself to feel this point as the centre of your being; this may sound or feel a little strange but bear with me.

Breathe quite deeply and softly into your diaphragm or belly. If you cannot breathe with the belly then do not worry as this will come with practice.

Breathe-in for about for 4 seconds if you can, hold for about the same if you can, then breathe-out for about 4 seconds. If you are hyperventilating then you need to breathe less deeply. If possible, do not breathe with your chest, just the belly.

Gradually allow the breathing to become gentler and less forced.

After 1-5 minutes you will notice your breathing is easier and softer. Now gradually let-go of control of the breath; just allow it to breathe itself.

Stage Three, Being:

Now, sit and be. Feel your belly and Hara as the centre of your being but do not concentrate on it.

As you sit and be, you may notice thoughts arising, memories appearing; feelings coming and going.

Do not try to eradicate or edit any thoughts or phenomena which arise or are 'seen'.

Allow thoughts, feelings and impressions to be; observing them dispassionately.

Allow all consciousness to be; without interfering with it.

If you get 'lost' in thoughts, feelings or other phenomena then do not worry as this is natural: instead, gently and lovingly bring the consciousness back, to Being here now, in this body, in this environment, in this Universe, in this Oneness.

Note that thinking and feeling are not 'wrong'. It is a common misconception in meditation practice that the mind should be completely empty of thought. However, the ego, which causes suffering, is not essentially caused by thinking and feeling, but rather by IDENTIFYING with thought and feeling and getting lost in them. If you do not understand IDENTIFYING yet, then please do not worry.

Just keep coming back to being here now and we are cultivating Pure Consciousness or Pure Self or consciousness beyond or below Ego Self.

Addenda; deepening the consciousness

If you are passionate about Self-Realisation then I would strongly recommend joining a good meditation group. In my experience, a good meditation retreat is highly valuable in deepening the awareness.

Please be careful about teachers, groups and organisations and use your intuition: there *are* good teachers but be careful if their motivation does not feel right.

Chapter Four

Truth, Being and Illusion

The New Age, Therapies and the Ego

As with most new endeavours in human kind, we are learning as we go along. So it is with the New Age: expansions in consciousness such as in the 1960's caused an explosion of experimentation in Being, some truthful and loving, and others dead-ends and egotistical indulgence. And this is happening now.

Many ideas then, are circulating the world, some truthful and some illusory and ego-derived. Many have been diluted or perverted so that people can bear to digest them. As with any field, the New Age has its charlatans and ego-maniacs and the aspirant to Oneness, Truth and Love should be careful of these as much as is possible.

Therapies frequently claim to be holistic, that is to treat the whole person, and of course they often serve a useful purpose. But they can also serve a very useful function in helping people who are uninterested in radical change and who instead prefer to alleviate their existential discomfort and ego-pain.

There are surely therapists who see the whole person and who deal in supporting radical beneficial change. Also, it may be that in some situations it is necessary to have a genuine therapeutic experience to let go of a particular 'problem'.

Why then do Jesus, Gotama Buddha and many other awakened ones seem to neglect dealing in therapy or patching-up people's egos? Probably because they are concerned with more essential, wider and more lasting change: with Universal Love, with Truth, with realisation of the Oneness of All. This is a change in the state of consciousness fundamentally, or a return to our natural oneness consciousness; not a patching-up of the same ill or perverted consciousness.

This is an important emphasis, both for the individual and for the world: radical change at an individual level (that is, abandonment of Ego) is the passion of Jesus, Buddha and awakened people. The world of Ego consciousness can be patched up a bit to make things a little better but at the root of Ego is separation, competition and selfishness; it is inherently damaging and redundant as we can see when we look at the world around us. This is because illusion and separation are at the root of it, at an individual level, thus bearing the fruit of separation, selfishness and ignorant action in the world, at a collective level. Gandhi I am told, said, "be the change you want to see in the world." This is starting at the centre, not patching-up things on the surface.

Therapies and New Age philosophies have their useful place; but for radical change or healing, that is for love and peace to be central rather than a nice quaint idea, they are not essential enough. Ultimately it is a change in consciousness in our being: letting go of Ego and learning to live in Oneness consciousness. Then Love, Peace, Truth and Oneness can be allowed to be in the world. This is a real possibility, (and not a foolish dream as ignorance or egoic consciousness would tell us,) and a possibility worth giving being, time and thought to.

Everyone is Awake. There is No Enlightenment

Essentially, concern for, or the seeking of, enlightenment, is vanity or ego or illusion. There is only one life it would seem (even if we see it as illusion, as a separated series of events.) Likewise there is one truth underlying and pervading all: the truth of our being, our existence.

What then do we mean then when we say that everyone is already enlightened or already awake? We mean that the awakened state is already here in our midst, in the centre of your Being, Now, as you read this. We may lose awareness of our infinite Being centred here now; we may forget about it, lost in illusory identification with desire, thought, feeling, memory or 'knowing'; but It is always Here Now, in the centre of our Being.

Thus 'seeking' is folly and vanity. Seeking, it would seem, generally, is a movement of mind away from our Pure Being, here and now. This is important to understand if we are to save both ourselves and the world from suffering caused by illusion and ignorance. The ego illusion tendency habitually moves consciousness away from this moment, here now in this Being, in this body.

To seek enlightenment is to move away from being here now. It is to move away from our natural , pure and perfect state: to move away from the Awakened or Enlightened state. Concern with depth of enlightenment or degree of awakening is trying to qualify the infinite and perfect beingness that every person *is*, whether they have realised it or not.

Few people in the world seem to value or recognise the awakened state of our being; in fact many view it as 'stupid' or 'slow' or even something to utilise for the ego-illusory tendency. Thus it is tempting to make proclamations (even in the Ego-field) to ensure people will take note of you and value the awakened state that you have realised and recognised. It may be that proclamations about depth or totality of enlightenment are at best moving one into dangerous territory and at the worst, high vanity. Possibly, some people have a pure motivation for making such proclamations but be very, very careful!

Conversely our Being should not be hidden – for it is infinite, perfect and immensely beautiful. It is there for all of us to love freely without attachment or limit.

It starts and ends here now in Us, in our being, not in any IDEA of enlightenment. There are no rules in being: it will Be as it Will Be; it is beyond mind and mind's ideas, though mind may come from it! By being in our Being, here, now, we will start to see the movements which the organism habitually makes into illusion. When Being, that is you and I, centred here now, observes illusion dispassionately then something happens: illusion begins to fall away as Consciousness comes home more and more profoundly to the centre of our Being here now. Practise Being Home with love!

Share it with others through life's joys, sadness and everything else (if you Will?)

Being in the ocean of Oneness is the original state. It is to come home and to look at yourself with love and compassion for your follies and well-intentioned mistakes in perception. It is to find Our true Self in love, and to share it with Us, with the Universe.

Living in the World of Opposites

It could be said that Meditation is largely a waste of time, if it is not applied to living in the world. What is the answer to the question: "how do we live at peace with our Self in the world?"

Assuming that we are not deeply at peace with our Self, then what do we do to find the answer? As you may have realised there are many people in the world claiming to give you the answer – and all in different ways: there is the New Age with all its therapies and schemes, there is philosophy and there is popular culture advocating materialism, make-overs, money and endless gratification and frustration. Oh, and there is religion in all its various forms.

However, as we may find from experience, we have to find it within our own consciousness: friends, teachers and wise ones may help show the way or introduce us; but being told the answer or knowing it within our intellectual mind is only pointing to the answer; eventually it must be EXPERIENCED and REALISED within our whole consciousness.

After time and effort perhaps, we realise the answer is not "out there". Rather it must go deeper and embrace all within and without. Here now. The truth is not an abstract idea but the reality of our Being, Now, Here. It really IS that simple. How then do we live? It's a matter of choice perhaps. And a matter of will. But most of all, a matter of Being.

The ego mind, by its nature, divides things. Division can be a useful tool. But it is a foolish Master. In fact, it cannot be the Master. If we are to find truth and peace. The mind and its divisions must be the Servant. Every aspect of our being, our consciousness, of the world, must be embraced with grace.

No matter how impressive or wise any philosophy or system of thought is: ultimately, it will be useless if we do not engage WHOLLY in the experience of existing here on the earth and embrace the whole thing fully, with openness and wonder. With "not-knowingness".

There is then, no path, no journey. There is no hierarchy of enlightenment, only Being, which embraces all consciousness within and without.

If we can be with all of our self and accept that self with dispassionate love – then we will realise once more that we are whole. And from that Wholeness, well what other way to be is there?

Living in Being, Letting Go of Ego

The awakened state is here now within us. As a rule of thumb however, it is essential that we are always careful. What then do we mean by "being careful"? Being, carefully, means always noticing. If we are careful and notice things as they occur in our consciousness, then we are less prone to losing our awareness of the purity of our Being.

To lose this awareness of the pure or perfect being is to fall into Ego or illusory consciousness. Staying out of Ego will save our Self and, equally important at least, the world, from unnecessary suffering and chain reactions.

Being aware and being, carefully, should not be confused with self-negation and self-flagellation, for these are ego-qualities. Illusory as Ego is, it will try to "own" spiritual matters if we are not careful! This is exemplified when one has an awakening or realisation of one's perfect nature in oneness- and then comes to a point of believing one is superior or knows it all now. This is why in Zen and mystical Christian teachings we are warned of the perils of being a "know-all". We can always return to Being and not knowing.

The Ego is Redundant

Oneness embraces all. If we are to enter into it then it seems that we must abandon Ego. Ego may be divine, if all is divine; it may have even been necessary. But its purpose is complete now. That purpose perhaps, is to allow realisation of our true Being. Now its job is done and it is redundant.

Ego is ignorant. It may *know* intellectually or be clever. But this is different. The realised person is aware of the suffering of other beings, not in a transcendental, metaphysical or super sense- but in a simple and profound way. Though this awareness is in all of us, it is often buried.

Ego is causing immeasurable suffering at a world level and at an individual level. It is very important to observe what is going on and to see what it is doing, both within us and without us. Letting go of it can be frightening to the illusory Ego but is joyous and liberating to the True Self that we are. Trying to hang onto it will cause suffering, illusion and chain-reactions affecting one's Self, and equally importantly, the world. What happens is up to us: we can compromise and have a bit of truth, a bit of love and ego; we can have all our nice New Age philosophy. Or we can decide, if we wish, that its time is done. It really is down to us and where we want to be at.

Usually in spiritual practice we see the attempt to serve two masters: Reality and Illusion, or Oneness and Ego. The world may need liberation from suffering, from greed, abuse of power, selfish distribution of wealth, torture, repression, killing and so-on. Though Ego may be illusory ultimately, it should not be thought of as a harmless necessity. For harmless is exactly what it is not. Nor need we get too serious or sanctimonious about it either, lest we feed the Ego-illusion.

The Danger of Knowing

Knowing is important in living on the Earth. If we do not know how to cross the road safely then we may die as a result. So knowing can prolong life on Earth.

As a young man at college, sitting in the coffee bar with a friend, Tony, I met an elf-like young woman. She talked nervously but with passion and showed me some drawings she had done. I looked at them and decided they were the work of a mad woman, still in her childhood. Though I was polite when I met her again, I 'knew' she was mad and quite deluded. I had also decided she was stupid.

One day, Tony took me to his flat and I met 'mad' Mary again. We began talking of consciousness, Zen and realisation. She offered me an assignment essay she had written, scrawled and with no punctuation. Reading it, I was amazed at her insight and the simple but profound wisdom on the topic. It spoke to me in a way that writings rarely do and shed light on areas new to me. Humbled, I felt so ashamed of myself that I apologised for thinking she was an idiot. I saw Mary differently after that.

Knowing or taking a viewpoint is not wrong- yet thinking we know how things are- can be dangerous if we are too sure of our own "rightness". Knowing can stop us from seeing the truth; it can close the gate so that nothing can come in. Can you see the potential danger in this? In meditation and in true dialogue, it should not be the master- only true self can be that. For the genuine lover of truth or Oneness "knowing" should be treated carefully.

Chapter Five

Seeing

The Seeker and the Short-Cut

Perhaps it will be found anywhere if one looks, and if finding it is more important than anything else.

Two itinerant monks had travelled far and long to see Boddhidharma. They sought counsel from the awakened one and he agreed to see them individually.

The senior monk came-in first to see him and disturbed by the frivolous decoration in the room, noticed a bottle of sakae on the table behind the master. "What holy man would harbour a liquor of illusion in his monastery?" He thought the baldy old man looked a bit slow and stupid: "is this the great Boddhidharma?". He told the master of all his scriptural learning and his prowess in meditation, his knowledge of past lives, his visions and his suffering as he searched for ultimate enlightenment. He had come far in his progress but needed now to know how to take his path further, to higher realms. The old man told him that his prowess in meditation was meaningless, his knowledge of past lives complete illusion, his visions mere ego and imagination, his scriptural knowledge of limited use and his path to enlightenment a fallacy, a mirage. The monk was most offended. But, the old man said, all was not lost, for his essential nature was Buddha, perfect, unspoiled and one with the universe. "Empty yourself of your ideas of how things are, abandon all desire for enlightenment, abandon all else except your pure nature," the old man advised, and all would be well. The senior left, angry.

The second monk entered with humility in awe of the great old master and a little fearful, yet to his surprise he looked a gentle man – not frightening at all. He noticed a stillness everywhere that seemed to vibrate with life and he told the old man of his travels and the holy ones he had met and of his fears and hopes. "This is it" said the old one, "it is here now as we sit; you are in Nirvana – only this, now, is the truth." And in that moment he realised it. All seeking seemed folly now and he laughed freely.

It will be found in Catholicism, in Hinduism, in Islam, in Atheism. But are we not tired, tired of the game, weary of looking? For those of us done with searching, done with games, then there is another way. A short-cut.

Awakening through Detachment

What does it mean to be detached?

To cultivate detachment we must first examine what it really is as far as Self Realisation is concerned. It is easy to hide in one's ego behind the banner of being 'detached' and this happens frequently in spiritual practice.

The concept of being 'detached' can become an unnatural one, that is, one involving the ego. Thus, perhaps it is safer to call it 'dispassionate observation'. What then does dispassionate observation require?

Firstly, relaxation.
Secondly, humility.
Thirdly, awareness.

As thoughts, feelings, desires and other phenomena appear to arise we need neither to attach (get lost in them), or to detach (remove ourselves from them). But we do need to observe without any viewpoint: we just observe.

Each person's character, nature and ego will differ of course, and some people will find it easier to observe thoughts dispassionately than feelings (or vice versa).

In short, we must be relaxed and loving with ourself. BUT WE MUST BE VERY CAREFUL IN OUR OBSERVANCE. We may be less aware of some aspects/distortions in our ego than others but it is ego which causes illusion, ignorance and thus suffering.

Clear simple observance IS AWAKENING.

Experience

The experiencer and the experience are, in truth, one.

Experience must be at the centre.

By "experience" one means experience of Oneness.

This is what is meant by "realisation" or "seeing" it.

If one is surrounded by materialism and shallowness then we may think about those things.

Put in an environment where one is surrounded by – love, truth, people living in Oneness, joy, sadness, life and death – and what would happen?

"Samadhi" is a Sanskrit word which means an absence of conditioned being:

Where we do not take our identity from anything specific; we do not take identity from a thought or series of thoughts.

In this state, if we take our identity from anything, then it is from being *one* with the whole of everything.

Nobody has a monopoly on this state.

Why have some people had a deep experience of Samadhi or Oneness? Does anyone really know? Does it matter? Some claim to know the metaphysics of it, but in the end will this help much, even if it is true?

The World of ego/greed/money and selfish acquisition is not interested at a profound level in states of Oneness – because, that state of oneness is a serious and profound threat to it.

Experience of Oneness is a birthright perhaps.

It is the time, now to get to the truth. To find out for ourselves.

That state is within our consciousness.

Anyone who perpetuates the myth that they have experienced it but that you cannot experience it (Oneness or Samadhi) in a month of Sundays, is a liar and a charlatan: for, how can they really know this?

Go into it and it will nurture you.

Munich – Monopteros, Englischer Garten

Sitting in the bandstand
Pool of water blowing in the wind
This moment now.
Beyond intellect/words.
Words are there, but not it/isness
This moment now is where life is,
Not in what passes for life.
It is at the heart, the centre, of this moment
And the centre of this moment
Is at the centre of One's being.

In that fullness, that infinity,
All artificial problems, worries, die;
There is only the Truth, in this moment.
When Falseness dies there is nothing left to restrict the
Truth, the oneness, the essence,
And the energy flows freely
And love occurs spontaneously
As we feel that oneness
In the stone,
In the bird,
In the person near to us.

Universal Self

Self and Universe are one
Universe is pure
Self is pure

Turn off the television and you can sense:
It is here
We are it
The gas fire roars quietly
Nothing is happening
Yet everything is here

Awareness is here
No effort
No doing
How beautiful
Oneness:
Trust it

Blue Empty Sky

All is gone
Striving abandoned
So much is here:
Infinity;
Self;
Being;
All is one.

What happened?
It was always here.
Only vision was concentrated,
Mind was looking out,

Desire was driving the vehicle.

But that is dead now
And in this moment:
Sky is blue and clear,
Mind has gone
And has dropped the reigns,
Self has gently taken them.
Self and Universe are One,
Freely held by love

Sky is clear,
Self is perfect and pure:
How bewildering
How simple

Drink Deeply

Drink deep from the cup,
Leave not a drop.
Abandon my morbid dialogue
Be:
Fully.
What is the answer?
        - I cannot say.
Words can only point to reality.

Have I seen God without form?
Only in you, me and everything.
Have I seen an atom?
Not yet,
though I've seen the shadow it cast.
Have I seen Ego in all its divisive glory?
        - It is not of the senses

What magnificent mystery of living
Engage
Choose not: this bit or that.
Embrace our being
In all its infinity.
Drink deep
And relish its wonder.
　　　- Oneness

Expansion of Consciousness

Expand our consciousness
Raise the vibration
Vibrating highly, hold it if you will

Being, perfect and pure
In Oneness
Opening hearts

Loving everywhere
Within and without

Oneness pervading all:
Form and formlessness
Coming together in untethered openness
In being, in love, in peace

In Oneness

Impressions

Thought impressions, like magic,
Layers flooding-in, in waves
What wonder of existence?

What's a feeling and does it matter?
What's a thought and do I know?
Except that it's marvellously too much
For my head to handle

If there are no impressions then what is there?

It's OK

Ah, here again
The purity of being, of life, of Oneness
How do we forget the purity?

How simple it is here
In the land of pure consciousness
Uncorrupted and incorruptible

Abandon the karmic field;
Come with me if you dare
To the land of Now, where all is pure:
Here

Ah, the relief of letting go,
Of all that shit:
'I' this and 'I' that
Of justifying myself and pretending I don't make mistakes
Of trying to follow some vain idea of what I thought I should
    be
Of pretending I am not vulnerable and inherently beautiful

It's OK
Whatever you have felt in this strange trip of life
Whatever you have thought, no matter how crazy, good or
    bad

Did you think you were the only one to think those things?
Or maybe, all along, deep down inside, some part of you
    knew:
That you are perfect and pure
But you could not listen to that still, small voice, so gentle
    and loving and asking of nothing

It's OK
Whatever you have done, good or bad
But to dwell on it is vanity
We were learning
And we've still more learning to do

Leave it all behind
Relax
Abandon the field of karma and illusion
Its time to be brave, to take a risky leap
Into not knowing

It's OK
Take that leap into that which we may never 'know'
And be safe in the bosom of the Mother, the Father
Oneness
Us

Noticing the Difference

Sitting
Back to zero
Consciousness is pure

A vantage point of not knowing
Notice how simple
One with Oneness

See the ego mind
Notice how complex, controlling and defending
Dividing and judging

Notice the difference
In energy, in consciousness
In strain

One holds us up in true self
The other, we hold up at great cost to ourselves
And to the world

This is the importance of noticing the difference:
One is pain and control
One is vital and nurturing,
At the bosom of Oneness

Noticing the Difference ii

Being is at home in infinity
Infinitely light and pure
 Nothing sticks to it
Stillness is at its centre
Ego is restless, two-dimensional
And heavy
Desire is at its centre it seems

Being

Relax, if you will
Let go of controlling
Allow all to be, if you will

Sit and be

And allow all to be as it is
To do what it has to do:
It works without effort

Relax, let go of guilt, unfinished desire
Return to zero
Where all is simple
Where separation is not at home
Where falseness must die

Relax: come home
To home in the centre of this moment
What is there here except Being?
Everything at home is being, magnificently
Bound together of its own accord by love so free

What was there anyway except being?
-just an illusion in our mind?

Chapter Six

Realisation of Oneness

One's Perfect Being

Being
Perfect Self
Pure in nature
Oneness embraces all gently
Without force

Realise it
Having realised it
Trust it:
The Mother and the Father

Remember it when one has "lost" it
Realisation is simple and whole
Realise it
Having realised it
Hold the reigns ever so gently
Working with the horse in harmony

How do we Realise?
And who can say really?
Through not knowing
And not through force
Through abandonment
Of one's own importance
Through love
Through Truth

Through Oneness

It pervades you, I, us
Oh how miraculous it is
How wondrous we are
Who can understand it?

Gone Clear

Gone clear
No karma (that I can see)
Mac has come-in to lie at my feet
No momentum now
No movement
Being is clear and uncluttered

How simple
How homely
Yet how miraculous we are

Mind Is Clear, Mind Is Pure, Mind Is Simple

Sitting quietly
Peace is here now
Oneness

Walking in Oneness
Mind is clear
Desire at rest
How beautiful:
People walking ahead, together

Birds singing, flowers being

Sun Shining warm
Air is cool

How simple
How profound
How gentle

You cannot grab it
You cannot 'know' it
You cannot force it
It does not shout
Yet it is always here

A way without a way
Beyond space and time
A way of the Truth, here now
A way of love

By the Lake

Sitting by the lake
With Joseph

Mind gone clear
I am still here
But 'I' has gone

Look into the lake
See to the bottom
How perfect, how clear, how one

See the fish so clearly
How miraculous

Mind gone clear like the lake
No splits
No this and that
Simple

Stripped of complexity
Of trying to do this
Of worrying about that
Of getting 'somewhere' for the idea of 'I'

How simple
Lost in unknowing and vastness
But home

One

All is One
Stop
Let go of knowing
It is here
Nowhere else
We are in Oneness
It cannot be divided:
Take the horses from the cart
And it won't go
All is one
All is good
In Oneness, nothing needs to be corrected
Trust it
Oneness

Being Pervades All

Music rings out clearly in wide empty space
Mind cannot make this moment
Cannot make the Awakened Being, being unmade in its
    nature
It can only imagine
Project ideas about some of it
Only Being in her completeness is
And mind is part of that
Oneness

Being Must Come First

In work, being should come first
And the work can be done without fuss and confusion

In love, being should come first
For pure love comes from being

In art, being should come first
Lest art only expresses ego

In speaking truth, being should come first
For being is truth

In Oneness, being just is
The ocean of Oneness, Being, is our Mother, our true Self
Trust it

At the Centre of Oneness

Walking, to the shop to buy biscuits
All is Pure

Wind blows strongly in the hazy
Sun between clouds

Thought flows softly in the glorious
Oneness

Here now, we are perfect

At this moment, vibrating highly

What miracle to be alive

Mac the old dog runs in the windy
Sun,

Laughing.

Chapter Seven

The World

Ego Is Necessary

The warplane has landed
Music plays as the line salutes
Someone has ended
How do his mates feel now?
How many thousands pass away unseen?
Now tell me: "Ego is necessary"
"It's illusion anyway"
"A little bit of Ego never harmed anyone"
Would his Mum understand?

Jesus, Buddha and Us All

Jesus taught love more
Buddha taught truth more
The world needs the two:
In Oneness

Love and Peace

What does the world need?
What do you need?
What do I need?

Oneness,

Love,

Truth,

Coming together,

Miraculous in our individual nature,
God meeting God,
Buddha meeting Buddha

Oh Jesus,
Oh Buddha that we are
And more.
Miraculous in our Oneness

Feel it in the sky,
Adore it in your shining sister of light,
Embrace it in your immaculate brother,
Seeing below the dross,
Vibrating so finely and highly,
Yet, without separation

Oh Self, Lord of all empires
Though owning nothing,
Great mystery of life and death
Sublime and beyond words,
Loving light from our being,
And words to carry us back home to being here now –
Where, the author that we are, lives

What do I need?
What do you need?
What does the world need?

Freedom/Problems

"Lord, how do you get out of problems?"

"I do not get into them"

The New Age and much of our current consciousness is concerned with sorting problems or improving our condition. Much of this arises from the illusory Ego and its desire to be in control all the time. Realising our true nature is not directly concerned with "control". In fact the Ego's control must be abandoned. The Ego, no matter what is said, will not bring freedom in itself because the nature of Ego is illusion, while Freedom is truthful and exists in Oneness.

The Ego, illusory as it is, would like to be in control, at the helm, dealing with problems or whatever else needs sorting out. This will give Ego enough to keep itself perpetuated.

The self realised one may have challenges that may even seem daunting but they are not made into problems at the Ego level. Surrendered to the Oneness, to Universe and True Self, deep down he trusts and knows in it, all will be well.

"Not as I would, but as you would Father"

Samadhi and Words

It's about a change
A change in Consciousness
It's about Being
The Being was always here I think
But we were looking out
Or looking forward
Or looking back

Sometimes we give up looking

I was thinking about how you can't put it in words

But words can point - so be open, if you will
And travel with me in Being, back to the centre

Transmission of truth
Of love
Of oneness –
It's not really by words
But words can be powerful

Words can point us to a place
And once we are there
We can transmit by Being, by love, by Oneness
By Being Together

Stay Open

Staying Open, one sees things as they are.
Priding oneself, on knowing how things are, lets nothing get
    past the gate.
Believe the wrong thing and it will close the gate.
Return to zero, to not-knowing, and release your burden.
Using one's knowledge wisely as required but knowing it by
    its nature: it is knowledge.
Staying open – and yet careful with clever ones who know all
    the answers.
Being, wary of falseness yet
Being in Oneness, with love.

Simplicity, Metaphysics and the Ego

Young Monk: Master, why do we have to wear clothes and eat
food?
Master: Just put on your clothes and eat your food.
    Being is simple in Oneness. There are many who claim to

know how subtle energy moves in the body, how the Karmic field works, how, metaphysically, the Ego functions or even what the primal cause of Ego is. This is a fascinating area but one which requires the utmost care and vigilance for the genuine seeker of True Being, Love and Oneness.

It is perhaps natural to be curious about such matters. Why then can it be dangerous? Firstly we can assume we know how we and the universe work physically. If we look at history we will see that explanations of how we or the world function are "relative" and thus subject to change. For example, many thought the world was flat. We may be right but we may also be proved wrong. Knowledge can save us from the undesirable but it can also serve the Ego or False Self.

Over the years we may meet those who claim to know about the nadis (subtle energy currents in the body) or the chakras (subtle energy points). This in itself is not a problem; the problem arises with involvement of Ego: if one is identified with Ego and the knowledge it has claimed, then we will not be open to experience Oneness. As soon as we think we "know it", we have lost it; lost Oneness that is.

Patanjali pointed-out in the Yoga sutras that there are three types of spiritual knowledge: that which is based upon book-learning; that which is inferred from another person who knows; and that which comes from direct experience. The latter is always the safer bet in my opinion.

As a rule of thumb, understanding subtle energy or how the chakras functions will not bring about radical change for the individual and the World. To the Ego it can be a great aid with which to selfishly indulge itself and take pride in its knowledge or metaphysical visions and avoid the realisation of Oneness and unfettered love. We need to get to the core, the essential, which is our Being in Oneness. Ironically, being in Oneness, we will actually start to see how things *do* work because we start to see without the judgement, distortion and preconception (that is, thinking that we already know it) which the Ego offers. This is seeing without trying. Or the direct perception or experience Patanjali was referring to.

Start with the simple then if you can. With our being, here now, in the centre of this moment. In Oneness, not in Separation.

Oneness and Fragmentation

Being is simple. Ego tends towards complication.

If we are to observe our self as clearly as it is possible, then it will help if we keep the process as simple as possible and this means in practice:

Just Being.

It does not mean just allowing the ego free reign; but rather a letting-go, relaxing and finding one's true self. From this vantage point we can see more clearly, and observe our existence, thoughts, feelings, reactions and so-on.

In other words, deep relaxation is combined with deep awareness and 'awakeness'.

It seems that the ego thrives on separation and fragmentation. Thus it helps to keep things simple. 'Just Being' provides an environment where the habitual patterns of the ego are observable.

If this observation is to be of any value then it must not be limited to sitting meditation or relaxation: the pattern must be broken and we need to leave as little room as possible for the ego to function in.

The conceptual mind of course, needs to separate things. This is not wrong or right; it is just a function of the mind. In spiritual practice however, the real Self (that we already are), must be Lord of all it surveys including the Mind in all its magnificence.

The True Self then, must be given priority if the mind is to function naturally and usefully. The Self if centred, or in its home, is in Oneness and mind can function purely in that

Oneness, even when it distinguishes one thing from another.

When we are not centred, when the True Self is not the master, then going into metaphysical complication can be dangerous as the ego seemingly rubs its hands together, excited at the potential for such fragmentation and separation with which to feed itself and keep its illusory self alive.

What Would Happen Without Ego?

Ego distorts the personality or character. Life without ego is simpler. The intellect can still function, only in clarity. The emotions are free to rise and fall or move.

We do not become an emotionless, characterless void or blank slate. When consciousness is pure we are in fact free to empathise more or become aware of our finer emotions, free to cultivate compassion. Free to develop our talents.

It is simply a letting-go of the 'dirty I' as Gurdjieff called it. And a release of our true nature, or true 'I'.

Seen in relation to the individual, letting go of ego is the beginning of an ever-opening flower. Seen in a world view, it is even more valuable. The world is sick with ego – and a radical shift away from ego and back to true being – is what the world needs. It may be of benefit to remember this in your practice. Awakening will be impure if it is just for the individual; it must be wider, purer.

The Art of Letting It Be

It will be as it is
This is not futility or desperation
It is the 'Way of Virtue'
Let people be as they are
Speak your truth as needed

If they change, they will change
Not by our will but from love
'Get the house in order
And the bigger house will follow'
Is it not by Grace?

Staying in the Centre with Love

Life continuously challenges us. Life does not adhere to a rigid set-pattern: it is infinite in its forms, its worlds and in its consciousness.

I think it is safe to say that ego consciousness feels at home with set, rigid and known patterns of thinking, and opinions and beliefs. There are certain ways of being we can use which starve this two-dimensional rigidity. These will be useful in meditation, and perhaps even more importantly, in everyday life and our interactions with others. These ways of being are many and not separate: they are in fact facets of one Being, in Oneness. Cultivating or allowing these aspects of Being will help us to stay centred.

Compassion and unselfish love have been advocated by mystics and sages throughout the ages. The World needs love desperately because it is an essential of complete and natural Being. A by-product of cultivating love and compassion is that, if applied 'across the board', it leaves little or no room for the Ego. It will also be worthwhile for us to meditate upon this and observe ourselves as we put it into practice.

Oneness and the Ego

We are in Oneness. The space or emptiness underlying the Universe, pervades all.

Living from the personal Ego usually excludes this universal truth, this universal consciousness. It is excluded because the

Ego is constantly and habitually referring all it sees back to itself. And this blocks awareness.

Realisation of Oneness or true meditation is the home-coming. Once home we need to nurture our Being by being watchful, always.

One thing to watch is the Ego's bid to centre, personalise or own all we are conscious of. For instance, "I think more than others do and it stops me meditating ..." or "my enlightenment is the biggest." This is the Ego's process of centering everything we think or do or feel upon itself. It perpetuates karma and suffering.

Buddha advised followers of the Truth to be mindful. Mindful of the formlessness pervading all form: underlying it all. We are in Oneness whether we realise it or not.

So Buddha advised we should be wholly mindful of our actions. If cycling for instance, we can be fully aware of the cycling. We may repeat the thought "there is cycling" as we cycle.

Being aware of the personalising is a powerful aid: we start to see the incestuousness of the ego.

It needs to be understood from within as the ego usually assumes that letting go of the "Personal" is eradication of personality. The practice of watchfulness only sounds the death of *false* personality or ego. It may sound confusing but ironically, realising one's true nature allows that nature and true personality to blossom. Healthy self-realised people are not walking empty shells – because as ego falls away so does it's restraint on the true personality. With practice we will develop a feel for what is true personality in our consciousness and what is Ego or false self.

True Being can then be seen in its shining beauty. And true being is in Oneness.

And awakening is the beginning of freedom, no longer for the individual's Ego but for the world, for humanity, for you and me.

For Us.

Truth, Oneness and the Ego

All definitions are by their nature limited. However we can define our True Self as the TRUTH. Oneness is that same Truth. We are the consciousness which is Oneness.

Ultimately perhaps, everything IS CONSCIOUSNESS. A good description of the true self is PURE CONSCIOUSNESS. What then is EGO?

Ego is, simply put, an identification with thought, memory or feeling. It is however compound in nature: it builds itself (it would seem) with each identification like a crystal forming from one small, simple beginning. The identification becomes so habitual that it becomes our 'reality'. It appears to take-on an identity of its own which can become very defensive, clever or aggressive when its identity is at stake. Though it appears as absolutely real, it is ultimately an illusion, a distortion of vision.

Patanjali said that the only purpose of the ego was to allow the realisation of what we are in Truth. Pure Consciousness.

As a rule of thumb, no matter how awakened you are, ALWAYS BE CAREFUL AND WATCHFUL. Ego can claim any experience as its own. But do not give it too much credence: it is just a distortion of perception.

Oneness at the Centre

If we have to pick the most important aspect in the spiritual life, then what will it be?

It is not in learning, in spiritual or metaphysical knowledge.

It is not necessarily even in spiritual practice – in being able to sit in meditation for hours.

It is in something which is at the centre of all these things;

something that embraces all these things.

It cannot even be described in it's entirety in words.

It is a change in perspective, a change in consciousness, a change in that which we are conscious of. Simply put, it is a realisation of Oneness and of our pure and perfect true Self.

The true Self, our essential nature is perhaps, always in Oneness with All.

At the very least, many people have experienced this.

Usually though, we are looking outside, so we do not recognise it. We miss it. We may be looking for something more important or dramatic: a new partner, a new car; or a dramatic "enlightenment". By nature, it does not seem to shout at us. It could be described as pure stillness, dynamic and in infinite flux. Most of these descriptions limit it or only describe one aspect of it.

But none of this matters because the answer is simple.

Normally the din of the ego mind takes up so much of our attention.

However, if we are still and watch, we will start to see the nature of Ego. More importantly perhaps, we will start to "feel" the obscure but profound real nature. This is our essential nature, called Buddha Nature of Christ Consciousness or True Self. It is "The Way of Virtue".

Frequently, the New Age movement is concerned with peripherals such as getting things we want or becoming more confident. These matters are not necessarily unimportant but unless they lead us to our true nature and realisation of it, they are like putting a quality "paint-job" on a car that is rusting from within.

Realising our true perfect nature must come before all else if we want relief from the constant nagging and sapping of the Ego or false Self.

We may think "enlightenment is unobtainable" or "it will never happen to me". It will not in my experience, happen how we think it should. This really, is illusion. All such ideas must be abandoned. For the "awakened" or "enlightened" state of being is already here within us. It is not outside. Nor is it to be found in the future. It is here now. In the centre of our being, in the centre of this moment. Essentially then, there is nothing to "happen" for this is illusion as it is more a matter of returning to our natural or pure state of being.

The world is in turmoil outwardly. Suffering may be illusion but that is poor consolation to one starving or being tortured. The world needs love desperately. Love on its own will not be enough. It needs truth as well. Both of these come from Oneness and the consciousness of it. Here, right now, is the centre point, in you, in me, in Us.

BOOKS

O is a symbol of the world, of oneness and unity. In different cultures it also means the "eye," symbolizing knowledge and insight. We aim to publish books that are accessible, constructive and that challenge accepted opinion, both that of academia and the "moral majority."

Our books are available in all good English language bookstores worldwide. If you don't see the book on the shelves ask the bookstore to order it for you, quoting the ISBN number and title. Alternatively you can order online (all major online retail sites carry our titles) or contact the distributor in the relevant country, listed on the copyright page.

See our website **www.o-books.net** for a full list of over 500 titles, growing by 100 a year.

And tune in to myspiritradio.com for our book review radio show, hosted by June-Elleni Laine, where you can listen to the authors discussing their books.

MySpiritRadio